Every Kinda Lady and Her Sisters' Pages

2020 Poetic Anthology

Edited by Nzima Hutchings

Every Kinda Lady and Her Sisters' Pages 2020 Poetic Anthology

Edited by Nzima Hutchings

Production Mgr. Nzima S. Hutchings, Every Kinda Lady Co.

Quill photo, Editor's profile photo by Rae'Kwon S. Robinson

Kevin J. Hutchings Jr., Assistant production Mgr.

Everykindalady@gmail.com   Instagram: Follownzima
everykindalady.com

Enfield, CT.

Printed in United States of America

ISBN: 9798622900570

Dedication

To all the women of these pages, thank you for sharing your narratives, voices, perspectives and candid thoughts...

In Loving Memory

A special dedication to my Grandmother Mary J. Campbell and my Auntie-Mom Linda J. Greene, who butterflied in 2020. To Knia Hutchings, my beloved daughter, that keeps me weeping on yellow flowers; I hope I make you proud. I will be forever your legacy and reflection. I love you all beyond words...

Thank you for being part of the powerful makings of me

Author & Editor

Every Kinda Lady Co.

Nzima states that her poetry, short stories, quotes, and expressive writing comes from life's upheavals; the hurt places, as well as the thankful, growing and feel-good memorable places. Nzima understands that it is impossible for her to live her life without accepting her whole self, married to all of her yesterday's thoughts and beliefs. The first line from her most requested poem, *Every Kinda Lady,* opens with "Constancy is an unfair brand of a lady." She declares that women wear several hats throughout their lives. It is unreal to hold a woman in one space or up to one light. She states that women wear a natural coat of armor; it is woven with all the fabrics and complexities of who she got to be, want to be and resiliency. Nzima says the truth is, most people find out who they are when caught in raw unrehearsed moments. Moments which fuel the awkward real truths about our authentic self, adding yet another layer and hat to our lives. Nzima has been reiterating, for over 10 years the Every Kinda lady Co. motto "make the important meetings with yourself," at every workshop. She has claimed it to be the first law of selfcare. Nzima believes one form of freedom is to write without shame or worrying about what others may think.

The Every Kinda Lady Poem, is the foundation of many things in her life and is the inspiration of the Every Kinda Lay Co. Nzima is an award-winning poetess for her work published in the 2009, Freshwater Poetry Journal; Expressive Writing and Literary Art Wellness Coach, Visionary and Sole Proprietor of the Every Kinda Lady Co. The EKL Company helps women to write their narratives, piece their life's puzzle pieces using their raw truths. This allows them to use writing for healing, balancing, mindfulness, legacy building and a means of self-care and relaxation. As, a graduate of Springfield College; a Connecticut Certified Sexual Assault Counselor, a member of The National Association for Poetry Therapy, and Community Advocate for Trinity Health of New England; her credentials and years of experience allows her to facilitate writing workshops for women and adolescent girls, including those that are victims of sexual violence.

Nzima's dedication to her community has not gone unrecognized. Nzima received the 2020 100 Women of Color Award, for giving back to her community as a Literary Wellness Artist; as well as, being the Visionary, CEO and Founder of Hartford's Literary Integrated Trailblazers (Hartford's L.I.T.). Early Publication of Nzima can be found in Nota Bene 2010 Phi Theta Kappa Honor Society Anthology. The poem was Untitled, but renamed Our Story. The poems "God Why My Flower Child" and "Eight" are published in the Freshwater Poetry Journal, under her former full birth name, Sherylle D. Roberson Hutchings in 2009, 2010. Current literary works and poetry can be found in the NBA Muslims, *Black Muslim Reads Anthology* and Hartford's L.I.T., 2019, and 2020 anthology". Nzima uses the Every Kinda Lady *Expressive Writing Prompts and Journal"* book: as part of the curriculum for her workshops. Nzima poetry books and journals can be purchased on Amazon, Barnes and Noble BN.com, or nzimahse.com

Published Works
Every Kinda Lady Expressive Writing Prompts and Journal
Every Kinda Lady" Monologues in Poetry (under first name only Nzima)
Poetry Café Spiels" an Eclectic Blend
We Be Two Word Poetry
Aishah and Nia Share Words (Arabic to English) a children's book

Journals (Nzima's Journal Designs)
She Wrote It…Then Spoken Worded it
My Red Book (red book/pages)
My Ladyhood Written Documentary (a guided narrative Journal)
Making the Importing Meetings with Myself
She Writes

Published Audio Podcast
Every Kinda Lady Café Hour
Apple Podcast, Spotify, Google Podcast, Breaker

Scan Me & Enjoy!

Every Kinda Lady and Her Sisters' Pages

Introduction:

The ladies of the, Every Kinda Lady and Her Sisters' Pages shared their innerworkings, internal monologues, poetry, candid thoughts, traumatic work throughs, resiliency observations, beauty, truths, experiences and tribulations. Poetic snapshots of their narrative are revealed unapologetically. Some of the pieces were birthed in the, Every Kinda Lady Co., workshops; such as Brave Space, Hand Me Down Roaches, Two-word poems, Private Party and others. In addition, several poems are included by author and editor Nzima Hutchings, including her signature poem Every Kinda Lady.

Mission:

The Every Kinda Lady Co. mission, is to strengthen women and teen girls' uninhibited voices, emotional wellness and emotional intelligence. As well as, provide empowering literary productions, guidance, and diverse platforms, for them to practice active acceptance and share their narratives using expressive writing, poetry, therapeutic journaling and a variety of healing art mediums.

Core Goals:

To help women write their narratives; piece their life's puzzle pieces using their raw truths. To encourage women to use writing for healing, balancing, mindfulness, legacy building and emotional wellness. As well as exercise and recognize the benefits of their uninhibited voice.

<u>Caution</u>

Note: This book is raw, filled with diverse experiences. The integrity of all the natural voices is accepted and celebrated…as it should!

Warning: If you are judgmental, one dimensional or skittish about curse words, sensual expressions, dark spaces, diverse religious tones then this book is not for you.

Original Lady

Accommodating Lady

Feminine Lady

Pioneering Lady

Feminist Lady

 Bag Lady

Angry Lady

Soccer Mom Lady

Single Mom lady

Peaceable Lady

Beautiful Lady

Fearless Lady

Liberated Lady

Balanced Lady

Nurturing Lady

Broken Lady

Ambitious Lady

Resilient Lady

Prolific Lady

Discerning Lady

Risky Lady

Submissive Lady

Hording Lady

Envious Lady

Wedded Lady

Poetic Lady

Compassionate Lady

Radical Lady

Classy Lady

Assiduous Lady

Spiritual Lady

Refined Lady

Confident Lady

Honorable Lady

Stupidly in love Lady

Powerful Lady

Egotistical Lady

Uninhibited Lady

Revengeful Lady

Subjugated Lady

Homeless Lady

Philosophical Lady

Mixed up Lady

Successful Lady

Depressed Lady

Proud Lady

Transparent Lady

Phoenix Lady

Naïve Lady

Abusing Lady

Pugnacious Lady

Renaissance Lady

Awakened Lady

licentious Lady

Ailing Lady

Modest Lady

Healing Lady

Stylish lady

Soulful lady

Merciful lady

Loved lady

Overworked lady

Single Lady

Eclectic lady

Giving to much lady

Imitator Lady

Desperate Lady

Militant Lady

Tired Lady

Haughty lady

Soft Lady

Caretaker lady

Chauffeuring Lady

Happy Lady

Young lady

Baby Momma Lady

Worried lady

Welfare Lady

Afro Centric lady

Humbled Lady

Acquiescent Lady

Diva Lady

Kept lady

Reticent Lady

Religious Lady

Human Trafficked lady

Divorced Lady

Gold digging Lady

Dramatic Lady

The other women lady

Status quo Lady

Vindictive lady

Promiscuous Lady

Needy Lady

Abused lady

Proud Lady

Bitchy Lady

Assiduous lady

Queen Lady

Walking in purpose Lady

Hurt Lady

Respected lady

Sistah-Mom lady

Discerning Lady

Injured Lady

Successful Lady

Polygynous lady

Creative Lady

Stupidly in love Lady

Visionary Lady

Obsessive Lady

Business Lady

Lemonade Lady

Judgmental lady

Skittish Lady

Fake Lady

Easily Moved Lady

Prude Lady

Conformist Lady

Every Kinda Lady

Surviving Lady

Vile Lady

Overwhelmed Lady

Confused Lady

Bad Bitch Lady

Worn Out Lady

Back-boing Lady

Supportive Lady

Procrastinating Lady

Leading Lady

Sexy Lady

Savage Lady

Realistic Lady

Hustling lady

Truculent lady

Renaissance Lady

Fearless Lady

Awakened Lady

Professional Lady

Tainted Lady

Suicidal Lady

Grieving Lady

Prideful Lady

Honorable Lady

Settling Lady

Girly Lady

Nipped Tuck Lady

Fatigued Lady

Every Kinda Lady

Constancy is an unfair brand of a lady

See I   I think I've been   every kinda   lady

her and her and   her too

The kind I   didn't understand

the kind I   feared envied   yet I   revered

the kind I   might've shamed   wouldn't claim

the kinda lady I   gotta be.

Yes, even that girl   her and her and   her too

The kind I   couldn't stand or   even forgive

The kinda lady that both lived   and survived

The kind I grieved   the kind I   I prayed heavily to be

The kinda lady I   gotta be

Yes,   every kind   even she...

Nzima Hutchings

The Every Kinda Lady Co. Foundational & Signature Poem
A testimonial poem of: A woman's acceptance of her whole self and the different hats
she wore/wears in her journey. Declarations of her unedited truths, self-governance, and
multilayered ladyhood are echoed powerfully...

Just Be Angry

Y'all act like Black Women woke up and said
let me just be angry with all these
awesome
mother fuckers around me
No rhyme or reason
just pissed because I'm melinated.

Tracy Caldwell

First love

He was her first love
that fist and kick kind of love

you know that hurt you cuz

I love you type of love

but she was his

and he was hers

well at least most of the time

when he wasn't cheating and he was always cheating

but she didn't mind

because she was that ride or die chick that I'm going to stick by your side

kind of chick

she knew he had needs

she believed she could Supply

he needed her for a punching bag

when he was sad or mad at the world for mistreating him

but she stayed yes, she stayed

because she thought she could fix him but at the end of the day she

couldn't fix him

she could only pay with her body

with her Bruises

with her tears

yet she stayed

because she could see things

others could not see

she could see all of his hopes and dreams and possibilities

she could see the weight of Life holding him down

she thought she could help him so she stayed

and she paid with her body

she paid with her bruises

she paid with her tears

this went on for years and years

until one day she looked at him

as if seeing him for the first time

she saw someone broken

someone striving to be something he could not be

a real man

she realized after all this time she was trying to turn water into wine

she realized after all this time he was tearing her down because he couldn't

get up

he was her first love but it wasn't love

Lashawn Henderson Middleton

Invisible Black Angels

Miss Miss Lady she'd say
help me get back to my good-good   and stay
help me get away   from my   body bartering   she said it done wore out

she'd cry   these-these   ashy bloody knees   and   pissy   warehouse
floors   kills   but the touch of the glass pipes   the smells n fumes
from burned spoons   street ruins   late night being invisible   while
pushing needles through   get me thru

the handover hand exchanges
the looking sideways and back   and over her boney   shoulders   gave her
numbs   and thrills   day to day

it's part of the high   a penance of such   the immense try
to escape her   unending broken heart   from whence
her father pulled her legs apart   she carried the blame in her gut
see it had come up   and spilled out when her lips parted
as she explained her   beginnings   and   endings

She'd repeated n replayed   and replayed n repeated her   claim
big eyed n halfhearted   *"I use to be a good-good girl   back in the day"*
momma use to say   until she died from being betrayed

Sadly, she never told me her name
she said it never been important   since eleven   people called her
Felicia   and overstated,   she hopes to never meet her

she said rest will do   to help her get back to her good-good and stay
we held hands   prayed   she closed her eyes   then   passed away
leavin   me a gift and a burden   the ability to see the most   invisible
America's ignored   Black Angels

Nzima Hutchings

I Need a $@#%ing Husband

A rat jumped out of the trash barrel and scurried across my hand while I was dragging it to the curb. I released a series of blood curdling screams. No one so much as peeked out the window to see if I was being murdered.

My throat is sore and my nerves are shot and bleach and scalding water were involved in the sterilization process. I have been performing this task joyfully. I see it as a celebration of being a capable, able bodied adult.

The moral of this story is: I need a $@#%ing husband.

Send eligible bachelors to my DMs. Please have two referrals.

Lynnette Elizabeth Johnson

Not to Fight the Breaking (Until We Return)

What if people felt it was okay to release more like clouds when it rains...

Not to fight to the breaking, but to let go when needed...

To refresh and renew

To appreciate what has been

To leave space for more

To nurture its continuance

To remember to take a next breath

And another

And another

As deserved

As planned

Until we return

Refreshed

Renewed

Sometimes we must cry

Stop to dance

Be carried along

Let our bodies be song

Play

Fall forward

Without plan

Just because sometimes

That's just the flow of life

And it's liberating

There are no sides

Everything just works

And rests

and leaves all to continue in whatever way it will

It's never too much

There is always enough

You can accumulate

But let go

Breathe

Be liberated

As it is in your nature

No matter what's around you

To be free

And flow

Like water

In the rain

Narelle Thomas

It's Complicated...

The reason why I have fallen off the radar with you is simple.
It's a me vs. me dynamic.
This won't be very diplomatic, but
Physically, I still want to f you.
Emotionally, I resent you for what has transpired between us.
I'd rather play no position, than the one that's on the table.
I'd rather hedge my bets, cut my losses, and stay in my lane.
I'd rather be true to ME and continue on, imperially.

It's so frustrating, because
All of this time we spent building something
A closeness, an intimacy, a bond.
All of this time, and I thought you really see me
For what I am.
I thought you were one of the very few who knew and appreciated
The beautiful multiplicity that is me
I thought you saw me.
Many people don't get to see me, but I let you. I knew you were special.
Correction. I thought you were special.
I gave you all of the benefit of the doubt, and figured that your status was
"it's complicated".
So, I allowed the space that would be needed to "un-complicate" things.
I didn't inundate you with probing questions and pry into the reasons why
I kept it organic.
I went with what came natural.
I surrendered to you and you let me
I fell and you didn't catch me
What the hell was that?   Who does that?
Who spends years on top of years chiseling a piece of wood
Mahogany, for conversation's sake.
To have that piece of wood transform and acquiesce, molded by your
hands
To have that piece of wood become completely enraptured by your soul
Completely enraptured. Completely.
Every other thought – completely.
Could not imagine loving you more – completely.
And what a waste. What a waste of my love. How out-of-line.
Someone who wanted "everything and nothing… all at the same time".

Roni D. Williams

The Message

Just be
Emotionally free
Be sad
Be mad
Be beauty
Unapologetically be
Exist openly
Express yourself
Blatant nudity
Of emotions
Publicly displayed
Pain sways
Tears tsunami
Leaving behind
Weak infrastructure
Brokenness uncovers
Abandoned fear
Leaves courageousness
Old mess
Makes new
Don histories
Like crowns
Past pain
Can drown
Not down
Look up
Great future
Flaunting gains
Two-stepping
Into possibilities

T'challa Williams

"Submission is Beautiful"

sometimes

sometimes life turns around

and completely shakes itself upside down

then I find

myself

on the left side

way - way - way

away from the side

that I thought looked as if it was

the right side

for me

it makes me angry

cause my intention is not to be lost in this world

you see

but I can't run in the dark

So, I have stop and notice every single leaf placed in front of me

and let it be that reminder that highs can't be high

without

those lows being low

So, In that moment

You see

one droplet of light is enough to illuminate the night

for me

even the playing field

sugar coat the confusion

yes, I know

things aren't the way things used to be

love ones have come and loved and now they are

so far

so far

away from me and the fulfillment of my needs

my wants

my heart

Lord, don't get me started

my heart

it's trying to mosey

along as the cod liver oil drips

from my battle wounds

Mama said it was best to heal

but it's not a armor shield against

the emotional turmoil

that plagues my soul

I can still feel its feet dancing

upon me

and I wish I couldn't

therefore I go

I go

trying to step to the sound of the wind

but what blows in

I find no real contentment in

you see

it's like going to your favorite store

and seeing the prettiest dress on sale

but still not having enough

to claim that name brand as your own

having enough is ideal

but this here is the real

reality

I struggle alongside the strugglers in the struggle

the bigger the plight

the harder the fight

the more I need to pray not to lose sight

and remain

away from the vain ones and

in the long run

I just want to learn to stand in the sun

and beautifully submit

to what was,

what is

and what will be

Maryam Sullivan

Bless the Woman

God-bless the woman
who has found herself
in spite of this tornado
called life
bless the woman
who is not afraid to just be unapologetically?
God-bless the woman
who sets the bridge on fire
with a vow to never look back
God-bless the woman who's mad at the world and everyone in it
wink at those who would judge her because they haven't got a clue
bless her dear Lord because you know what she's been through
bless her when she curses
bless her when she lies
Bless her dear Lord
wipe the tears from her eyes
bless her because you know like your son she's been crucified
bless her in her foolishness
her craziness too
bless her dear Lord when she blames it all on you
Lord you know her heart like no one else can
bless her dear Lord because you understand
Lord bless the woman who still knows she needs you
bless her and keep her lord in all she goes through

Lashawn Henderson-Middleton

Which Box?

Which box are you forced to choose?
What if none applies?
What if they are all lies?

What if I am both African American and Hispanic?
What if I am Native American and Hispanic?
What does it mean to be Hispanic?
Do I hail from Spain or Latin America?
Who speaks Latin? Sigh....
So which box do I choose?

If I am White, what does that mean?
Where is the White country?
Who gets to be White?
Can I be white if my skin color is olive tone and I do not come from
Greece, Turkey, Italy, Spain, but look like I could be?
I am so confused!!!!
Which box do I choose?

How do I choose if I am from Hawaii or Samoa, or Papua New Guinea??
What if my people are indigenous? Meaning my ancestors are the mixture
of
The Moors who came here with Abu Kari Mansa and became the Moorish
tribes?
The same ones you call Seminole, Cherokee, Cree, Creek, Muscogee,
Chickasaw, Yamasee?
What if I am a decedent of the Iroquois Confederacy which include the,
Mohawk, Onondaga, Oneida, Cayuga, Seneca and Tuscarora? Are we
Native Americans or inhabitants of Turtle Island?

What box do I choose? Did you know that this land mass belongs to
Morocco? Did you know this land is under the Treaty of 1787? So which
box do I choose? Whose country is this really? Is the Red, White, and
Blue flag really the flag of this country? Is not the Red Flag with the
Green Star the true Flag of El Moroc Al Aqsa? Always present but never
shown?

Where is the box that says Moor?

El Moroc is stolen land. Before 1492, there were no jails, mass crime, warfare which killed women, children, and elders. Before 1492, our numbers were great. We were enslaved before the Africans came, we were burned out, starved, kicked off our land, moved to unknown territory, belittled and stolen from our parents' arms and sent to boarding schools to take away our heritage and our names. How did this happen to such a land of many nations who lived peacefully for the most part? The Hindus came, the Chinese Moors, the Tartars came, the Olmecs came, the Vikings came, the Malian Moors came, the Negritos came. There was no wholesale slaughter of human life. Migration took place and towns and communities were formed, trading took place, allies established all without killing every man, women, and child.

Which box do I choose? Who am I really?
Choose one. Or choose other? What does other mean? From another country, planet? Am I the Other?
Which box am I forced to choose?
What If none applies.
What if they are all lies?
A fabricated construct that benefits a group of people who steal, rob, rape, murder, and rule with weapons of mass destruction and lack of morals.
So, which box are you forced to choose?

Na'imah Muhammad

Americans-especially the White

Americans--especially the white ones-- admit it. We are at that point where you are at the family reunion and you realize 'Wait a minute. Why we doing this? These folks are way too old to effectively force us all to do all the same ole things we have been doing for years. Time for change!' And then you boldly declare that YOU are running things next year and everything is going to be upgraded, bigger, better, more youthful and fun--maybe even catered and a family app, definitely an app--because that's how things are SUPPOSED to be! After all it ain't 1979, its 2020! And next reunion comes around and you realize just exactly how much time, energy and money your fancy plans are gonna cost you and NO, Auntie and Madea ain't helping because they pissed off at you for wanting to change things in the first place. That is where we are right now America, if we are being honest. This thing can go, 1 of 2 ways. And either way ain't gonna feel that good for somebody. <---coming from a woman who thought it was a good idea to serve chowder at the reunion she hosted, just because we were having it at the shore. People be like "WhereDaMacaroniAndCheese"?

Amalita Van Buuren

I'll be Your Blackie (Blackie defined)

Blackie is **B**EAUTIFIED audaciously, balance in the galaxy the epitome of unapologetic femininity

Blackie is **L**OVE, modesty, warm fires... shining stars

Blackie is **A**LL natural...feared.

Blackie is **C**LEVERNESS cultivated, chakras energies n hues, dark n light Powerful!

Blackie is **K**EMETIC life's symbol, ethereal fruitful gardens.... envied, revered, and bitten

Blackie is **I**ndigenous Queen mothers and daughters

Blackie is **E**VERYTHING

Nzima Hutchings

Hand Me Down Roaches

Hand me downs

and frowns

Want my own

But folks say wait till grown

Yet, the groans of growing pains

Cloud my hearing

I'm not seeing

Distracted

Like, when a roach is on the wall

You wanna say

Or spray

Take action!

But you not moving

All the thoughts give anxiety

Why am I fighting me?

Or perhaps

Its

These hand me downs.

These, clothes I found

Cloaked in another

Even my brother

I want my own

Black people have

A right to own

But

All I possess

is hand me down mess

Other people's stress

Frustration press

All because, I'm not wearing my own flesh

Possessing my own space

Looking in my own face

And

only

seeing

me

I don't care what it takes

My freedom is at stake

My dreams are not hand me downs

And these ain't my roaches

And imma spray and slay

Anything that encroaches

T'challa Williams

Original by Design

chocolate   butter pecan   tan

Asiatic   blue-black hues

woolly soft fro   kinky curly locs

styled in Harlem's tracks n blocs

crochet   bantu knotty knots

ponytails   cornrows

smellin all   organic   like

coconut n   Jamaican castor oil,

even blue magic n African royal.

wit soul connecting window views

ranging from hazel brown

to midnight blues

ain't nottin but God's truths

natural feminine stance

dominant n swagger

rhythm refinement   prolific

poetically timed   intense

flawlessly complete

carryin the original   woman   design

made by the divine   divinely

a Black Lady she be

Nzima Hutchings

For Barbara

Sister, how you stay so sweet?
I've heard young brothers as a girl, "Sugar, how you get so sweet?"
Gettin' sweet is baby business, we come here sweet.

Stayin' sweet is a wonder

Sweet through the truth of the cruel lies you've been told
Sweet through the contradictions and chaos that raised you
Through the rapes that should have ruined you
The tears nobody wiped,
Sickness nobody tended
The babies you bore and raised alone
Sweet through the choking poverty that slapped you and laughed
Sweet through hunger
Sweet through betrayal, abandonment and abuse-in your black home and
white world
Through the hatred of your kind
The subjugation of your whispered breath against the screaming racism
saying you *don't* matter
Sweet when rejected, failing the brown paper bag test
Holding up the wall at the dance

You are sweet tea for my life, brown, fluid and satisfying
Rocking in the front porch swing sipping sweet with a warm kitten in my
life

Can you teach me?   My sweetness is waning
Giving way to remorse and resentment
Curding, cursing and crying, drying up and dying

I beg you to tell me
Sweet matriarch
How you *stay* so sweet?

Regina S. Dyton

The Greatest

I
Maybe worse than the raging and cursing, the secrets and scary nights
when your key turned in the door to unlock my nightmare

Maybe worse is what you never did
You never read me a story
You never rocked me to sleep
You never twirled me around
You never told me I was pretty
You *never* told me I was pretty
You never told me I was pretty!

You never told me I was pretty, not once in 21 years! And then you died.

You told me my hair was nappy while laughing the question, "Who is yo
pappy cuz yo hair sho is nappy?"
You called me Topsy and thought I didn't know her; I knew she was black
and ugly like me

Like me!
Black and ugly like me
Black and ugly like me
Like me! Topsy is black, fat and ugly like me!

You called me butterball and Eat Mo' so I always thought I was fat-100
pounds ago I thought I was fat, thus fulfilling the prophecy.

Maybe if you did that sometimes to tease but at other times held me safe
and close,
Other times sang me songs, tucked me in
Instead of sneaking in after I was asleep

Shared a hot dog and a soda on the porch
Told me I was pretty
Told me I was pretty
If you thought I was pretty?

Told me to smile because you wanted to take a picture of me in my puffy
dress
Let me dance on your shoe tops
Spun me around while we both laughed
Chased away the nightmare beast
If you loved me

If you ever loved me at all
I might
Have had some foundation or standard or clue
Of what the hell to do!

I might believe in an all loving father God- *I don't.* I recoil at the thought!
No daddy, the God I serve has a big, thick book of jobs for this servant
you sired

Working for every breath
All to earn a crap shoot at survival

And I've been afraid of every man and woman I've ever loved and didn't
love but laid down with out of fear

While they judged me a Jezebel,
Sin in sepia

Black and dark
Only me and these thoughts
Taking shallow breaths
Into panicked sleep
Awaiting assault
Waiting for the second shot: the lie in the morning from mommy.

"That sounds like a real bad dream. Just say your prayers and know that
God is with you."
I don't know!
I know that the devil came in and bit my big toe
Somebody shot me
Right between the legs!
Look at this scratch, this bump, this bruise

"It's probably just from you wetting on yourself"-You left the sheets on the bed all week until laundry day, intensifying my feelings of filth and disgust

My left breast hurts because somebody put a bullet in it and pulled it out by a string like a tampon.

I knew you wouldn't believe that one and I was finished talking to you by that age.
If you had been able to listen and hear, maybe I would believe or even trust my experience, perception, intuition and judgment

I don't, at least not yet

I have deemed myself unqualified for love.

I don't know how to screen them, don't know how to take care of myself in relationships
I freeze upon the absurdities of assault as it works its way through my body,
Chokes my throat, snags on my heart, smothering my lungs. It balls up, congealing in my stomach,
Quivering

But not as much as before

If nothing else, my father made me strong and independent, not willing or able to depend on anyone-financially

I see now that I did depend on him for validation of my femininity, value, beauty, desirability and worth. And later, I depended on a man for it, and a woman and my good work for it.

I worked and studied and studied and worked and worked some more; emotional work, spiritual work
Homework to find my way home

A little l further down the road I'll meet sweet Gina, rocking in the sunshine, singing in the rain, showering in a waterfall, innocent again

As clean as if you never touched me

Confident as if you never raised me, as if you never made me
As if I had been loved
by The Greatest

II
But that some man would be big and strong
and want to take care of me

My fantasy father is Muhammad Ali

His greatest feat
Is to fathom how sweet this baby girl
This sweet baby innocent pretty little girl
He makes me know I have it
That sparking bright light that
Makes people look at m and say, "Aaaww"
And tickle my belly with raspberries
And cuddle while we sing together

Until he sings alone

Because she is sleeping in his arms

Long after the world has rejected, abandoned, betrayed or just forgotten
him
He will always be

Her champion.

Regina S. Dyton

Out of Sight but Not Out of Mind

Oh, listen to me

Echoes in the night

Sweet tone of voice, I hear after the fight

Oh, listen to me

Hear me out

I'm sorry, I hit you

And laid you out

Your eye glistens

The swelling making you lose your sight

It's only for now

Temporary, he says

Listen to me

I won't hurt you in anyway

I can't see you like this

Give me a kiss!

So, we can make this better

We just need some prayer

It will be better, later

Can you hear me baby?

I'm sorry, can you forgive?

Even though you made me do it

We'll get through this

Cause our love is strong

Hey you were wrong

Just had to prove my point

What I say is what goes

You need to stay in your place

That will prevent the aches

I can't bear to listen

It's making my heart stiffen

Making the love that I had for my father

Diminish

Does he understand

You can't look up to a man

Dat lays his masculine hands on the QUEEN of your land

Oh, LISTEN to me!

I won't ever understand

How you "love" her during the day

But before you lay

You bring her so much pain

You're a fraud

Outta my sight

But not outta my mind

You're just a coward at night

Beating on your wife

La'Mora Hardy

Woman to Woman

Release all those bags

listen to the lady

name

Conscience

that sits heavily on your shoulders

ranting and raving

about your needs.

Shake off the past damages…

Inhale new possibilities…

Reach around

to the nape of your neck,

grab your spine

and pull it up

Watch-out

faithfully

for everything will

fall into

place…

Nzima Hutchings

The Way

This is The Way to be Yourself

To open Your Heart

To know How

Authentically Real You are

Accepting Your flaws, Your wrinkles, and Your jiggles

Loving Your fat ass and floppy titties

Knowing Your instinct is Who

You want to be in company with

Surrounding Yourself

In the space of those who

Also know

Are aware

And care

This is The Way

To be open to Yourself

Closing out the past

The pain where?

Back there

This Is The Way to be Yourself

IfeMichelle Gardin

I will not apologize for being a "Bona Fide Bitch"

As days get older each and every night grows colder, If I don't satisfy your "Itch" oh how easily you quick to call me a BITCH.

Yes, I was that "Bitch" you needed quick, anytime it had something to do with your dick! Now ain't that the pot calling the kettle black, you see it takes A "Bitch" to know A "Bitch"

I would stand by your side feeling any moment I would die, the tears I would spill felt quicker than A Hitman's kill

You mothafuckn right I'm A "Bitch" make that A "Bona Fide Bitch".

Stephanie Alexus

<u>Synchronicity</u>

music and poetry

like parallel playin girls

with new formed breast

drumming up on

yesterday's mysteries

rhythm   and blues

bars   meters   rest

Nzima Hutchings

A Black Woman, A Black Mother

Well, son, I'll tell you:

Life for me ain't been no crystal stair.

I AM A BLACK MOTHER, I live in constant fear of my child being the next name that is shouted through the streets, as a force in the movement for the lives of others.

Like Sandra Bland, Breonna Taylor, Shante Davis, Fannie Lou Hamer, Amadou Diallo, Trayvon Martin, Tamir Rice, Botham Jean, Amad Aubrey, George Floyd, and Emmett Till!!

We say their names, say their names, and say their names!

All born from the wombs of Black Mothers like me

Black Lives Have ALWAYS MATTERED!!

Why is it such an unreasonable expectation for Black Mothers hope for their children to live in the pursuit of happiness without fear of being assaulted for being who we are!

For Being, For living.

It's had tacks in it,

And splinters,

And boards torn up,

And places with no carpet on the floor—

Bare.

I AM A BLACK WOMAN. I have dreams, aspirations and goals to reach.

I'm tired of being sick and tired. I'm DONE with being the strong Black Woman for everyone I'm not claiming this box of titles you put me in. I shall no longer be boxed in

Life for ME ain't been no crystal stair

I AM A BLACK MOTHER I want my babies to live full and complete lives. Having faith that there is no concern for their lives every day. For my son to jog or eat ice cream on his couch. For my daughter to sleep peacefully in her bed to drive to work with her music playing loud in her car. For my child to play in a park

Black Lives have always mattered. I am responsible for bringing forth all the Black Lives on the Planet!

I'se been a-climbin' on,

And reachin' landin's,

And turnin' corners,

And sometimes goin' in the dark

Where there ain't been no light.

I AM A BLACK WOMAN. I've cleaned and I've cooked and I've made a way out of no way for so long. I'm not as strong as you say I am; I just know how to make it look dam good! Despite humiliation, scorn and contempt for my people. And Still I Rise

And reachin' landin's,

And turnin' corners,

And sometimes goin' in the dark

Where there ain't been no light.

I AM A BLACK MOTHER. I know the worth of my babies. I pray, every day I breathe, the systemic oppression that has plagued my people for so long will not cause another Black child to harm my child. I pray every day I breathe, the system of oppression doesn't stifle, suffocate and kill my child

So boy, don't you turn back.

Don't you set down on the steps

Cause you finds it's kinder hard.

Don't you fall now—

I AM A BLACK WOMAN

I stand, when my feet hurts, my back hurts and my spirit is challenged! I

persevere, when I sit in the front of the bus after a long work day, I

persevere, when I am abused and used at work, at home and in society

For I'se still goin', honey,

I'se still climbin',

And life for me ain't been no crystal stair.

I AM A BLACK MOTHER

Black Lives Matter because I matter. I am responsible for every Black

Life on the planet. I am the force behind the movement.

I AM A BLACK WOMAN – I AM A BLACK MOTHER

IfeMichelle Gardin

I Wasn't Ready to Let It Go

Not now probably not ever
It was a love that motivated me
A love that moved my soul
A once in a lifetime kind of deal
That real, raw, and relevant kind of feel
The kind of feel that leaves you
Stuck dwelling in your feelings
Swirling with confusion and doubt
Self pity and despair
It should of been me
It should of been us but
Not at the expense of another's heart
It was a love that changed me
A love that met the desires of my heart
Real, raw, and authentic
A wise man once said
Timing is everything but
I ain't ever watch a clock
I wasn't ready to let it go
Felt like I had only scratched the surface
Of what could have blossomed into
Something sweet and savory
It was as if you walked out of a dream
Out of my dreams
I envisioned giving you my all
Building a life together
My reality was distorted
You had me thinking like a naive 16 year old
Before rape, sexual assault & domestic violence
You brought me back to a hope filled place
I wasn't ready to let it go
The taste of your lips on mine
The warmth and care from your affection and attentiveness
I just wasn't ready to let go but
It's hard to hold onto something so precious
When you belong to someone else
Life's got me feeling like I'm merely a possession
Lock stock and barrel
There was never a need to pull a trigger

For the first time in so long I was feeling
Heart racing
Butterflies in my stomach
Choking on words
I was feeling
Experiencing passion
Giving in to my desire
I ain't ever been high but
I was high on you
Smoking on your essence
Every day in every way
I wasn't ready to let go
But now I understand
Just because you love someone
Doesn't mean you always end up with them

Doc Poetic Jewels

Cathartic Releasing (for Sr. Anyango)

arched spines
temperatures *high*
quivering thighs
moisten backs-n
panty lines
booty twisting
formation lines
caramel stretchin
chocolate warmin
vanilla creamin
curvy-n skinnygirl
pipe dreamin
Afro-n Latino
Sheroe swags
Synchronized   swinging
baggy sags
attitudes-n egos
don't care
flirty eyes
wry grins
got   this
fuck   this
furrowing eyes
body cries
"we ain't
die   yet"?
heavy breathin
glistenin limbs
pumping breast

locs flowin
Sistah Lady
killing zumba
kissin chakras
exposing colors
yelling out
Ohhh yeahhh!!!

five   four

three two
level up   level up
wind downs
n   cooldowns
thanking heaven
we got
old skool
two steppins
finger poppins
bottled water
Marvin Gaye's
let's get
It on
"If the
spirit moves-ya
let me
groove ya"
grown lady
body expressions
n transformational
facial muggins
owning **you**
coming through
connecting to
India Arie's
Private Party
self lovin
and life
balancing rendezvous

Nzima Hutchings

Suicide

Days when I decide perhaps, I'll try suicide

I think who will hug my babies n grands like I

Days when I decide perhaps, I'll try suicide

I think who will be able to set *my* table

Days when I decide perhaps, I'll try suicide

I think who will care for my tea garden

Days when I decide perhaps, I'll try suicide

I think who will keep my hubby company

Days when I decide perhaps, I'll try suicide

I think who will remind my father he gave me power

Days when I decide perhaps, I'll try suicide

I think who will take the photo

Days when I decide perhaps, I'll try suicide

I think who will wear yellow for my daughter

Days when I decide perhaps, I'll try suicide

I think who will answer my sister cuz call

Days when I decide perhaps, I'll try suicide

I think who will ask my creator to have mercy on me

Days when I decide perhaps, I'll try suicide

I think who will shamelessly throw my Nina Simone piano away

Days when I decide perhaps, I'll try suicide

I think who will make the I'm sick tea for my family

Days when I decide perhaps, I'll try suicide

I think who will get in a teacher's behind about mine

Days when I decide perhaps, I'll try suicide

I think who cares what others think

Days when I decide perhaps, I'll try suicide

I think who can help me with these new-fangled thoughts

Days when I decide perhaps, I'll try suicide

I think who the hell am I kidding I been here before

Days when I decide perhaps, I'll try suicide

I think who will tell the other ladies in me, to keep fighting for me

Days when I decide perhaps, I'll try suicide

I think who will not forgive me for stealing time

Days when I decide perhaps, I'll try suicide

I think this maybe the worse day, but can't be everything

Days when I decide perhaps, I'll try suicide

I think who but me could set me free

Nzima Hutchings

Hijacked by Grief

In a cloud where only, she thought she lived.
Selfish to think she was that special and no one else could relate.

Selfish to think no one would understand.

20 years later the cloud began to disappear.

After meeting Honey B…..She started to share.

She began to breathe, and started to heal.

That time she realized how blue the sky was….

That time she realized how the birds flew in accordance to.

That time she saw HER.

She is beautiful along with all the rest of GOD's creations.

HER frowns turned into smiles.

HER heart remained pure as gold.

HER mind, well HER mind unmatched.

HER soul...no other like it.

I am his Daughter.

I am her Mother.

I am HIS QUEEN.

Watch HER.

Pray for HER.

Love HER..

TODAY STANDING FIRM WITH My feet planted.

TODAY not falling for the BULLSHIT.

TODAY I CHOOSE TO LIVE LOVE LAUGH

TODAY DONT MISTAKE HER KINDNESS FOR WEAKNESS.

YOU will respect HER.

Today I say Hey world, remember me...

The one in the cloud, who started on the ground.

The one who had so many dreams and aspirations.

The one who FORGOT about herself.

No longer IGNORING her intuition…

No longer afraid to speak her TRUTH.

No longer putting herself LAST.

I'm filled with GOD in my Heart and mind.

I'm BOLD.

I'm Courageous.

I'M HERE...

I'M PRESENT...

I'M READY...

Letting go and flying free.

Unapologetically ME.

Elizabeth Shaniqua Johnson

Sincere Intention

Is it the same as wishing upon a star
Can it be used as an excuse to remain distant
From That which lies within and is only known
To the Creator, all that is great and small

Sincere Intention
Can it exterminate the evil that lies within
Or clear the soul and heart of unspoken sin
Maybe It can guide one to the true purpose
That is Bound in purity and hope

Sincere Intention
Is it about Accomplishments in this world
Some by design, some on a whim
Our feeble attempts to produce with our own hands
What the Omnipotent knows of in advance

Yet when we see the outcomes of all things
The Good and the bad
There is an understanding
That nothing happens outside of His plan

Sincere Intention
What really is our purpose
Can we follow the path that looms ahead
And commit wholeheartedly
Without hemming ourselves in

Sincere intention
Accepting all that one becomes
As a part of the creator's plan
A future filled with potential
That is waiting for you to stand
In your place among the living
Being one who accepts what is and what can't be denied

You Have to decide if life was meant
To be lived for the desires that distract and dissuade
Or live for the eternal that takes all intentions into account

Remembering those loins that birthed us
And those warriors who took the blows for us

Sincere intention
Calls for remaining steadfast on a path
To reclaim our truth as children of the earth
Pursuing higher realities that create a breath
Of fresh thoughts and designs
That allow for peace and tranquility
Witnessing our rise above the fragility
Of this life in order to utilize
Our strength from within
To begin again

Jamilah Rasheed

I Am Beautiful

I am BEAUTIFUL
Let me say that again

I ...AM ...BEAUTIFUL

With all my imperfections
with a heart that loves so deep
And climbs so steep...
Over mountains and barriers,
created by a world sometimes, unforgivingly cheap

Passing out bills
but then saying
they are not yours to keep ...

I AM BEAUTIFUL

With a mind so creative
And dreams that can take over the world
With a soul that cares
for everyone that dares
to enter a life that's been seasoned, with trials and tribulations,
and tears of agonizations   turned
into a beautiful rainbow

so in conclusion my dear sister -
Let that spirit GLOW
Don't hide, rather SHOW
the World, what an unstoppable force you can be
as you learn to
LET GO

Because...
You
ARE
BEAUTIFUL

Yes, You Are Beautiful

Asmaa Kamara

Faithful Sister

I see the beauty of Islam in you

I see it in your works of compassion, love and generosity

In your welcome to all you encounter

Your wide, white, slow smile emanates from the depths of your dedicated soul, intelligent mind and the way you greet me as your sister

I see my own beauty reflected in the peace of your eyes

Allah has apparently healed and continues to heal the wounds of American racism and sexism

The devil authored narrative that says we are too dark, ugly, nappy, fat and bossy

The troublesome Western tale that values us as objects but not as people- Nigger wenches good for one thing that comes in many forms-rape, name calling, beating, lying to us that we are evilly tempting and at fault for the assaults

No. I'm not naïve. I know full well that men of every ilk in every society abuse its women. I'm talking about *you* most beautiful woman who knows herself. *You* who's study and worship bears plentiful fruit

You really said something when you said "My naked body belongs to him who first falls in love with my naked soul"

The words of a sister at peace with herself and her God. I get some of that peace each time you greet me with your loving embrace.

Regina S. Dyton

The Block

I'm driving down our street bowing my head at the threads of balloon
candle shrines along the way counting and taking a soul a day...memories
A guy steps out from his stroll with a pole holding a sign deep in his grind
it read "I'm selling good karma", I shrugged and dropped a coin hoping to
buy some for me and him
mostly me wondering always how could this be

I left a place where a lady hung low kissing the ground while her kids
hung around ...what dope of trade would have her degrade
her-self
Lifeless,
self-less yet selfish
kids left for doom ...

Shouting out like sonic booms "damn girl! That ain't ya hair! And he ain't
ya daddy neva was! Fling back strays of plats loosening at the scalp.
Looking like mops of yarn matted and patted, money's short.

Money's short but he be about that life...wading on corners night after
night. Slinging and stashing
...momma' got to put out. Dreams broken long ago.

Crumbled tissues lined his pockets life's years lined his cheeks so the tears
could always find the tracks and the tissue he used to wipe...wipe them
away as if..as if with each wipe were the years and oh not to mention the
tears wasted cause they couldn't help him face it...hey you got a quarter?
That phrase on constant rewind...here's to life..his tee shirt read...I am the
future

Parables when life ain't really life mirroring its dark twin ... but why death
gotta be dark? Maybe it's light, maybe it could make this imitation of life
...right.

Red white and blue stripes, and a single star - selling futures for dreamers
in the form of green furry whispers, the skin of kiwi the flurried sweet soul
of mango! Yo 'momi' you want to buy? Ici, coconut plantain! That face of
brown gold ...sigh ...when I denied to buy..the muffled whispered
NEGRO...negero

Man please
ageless smiles or upside down frowns grace the medleys of blended yet
living a part like cast out castaways all brought here or dropped there
serving purposes of willie lynch knots
still no pot of gold or 40 acres neither… we're the mules.

HEY you wanna buy this paper or not?? Snapped back by local
realities...ok, just give me 20 for this EBT, stash...you get 50...I need the
cash.

I turned the corner now my smile is upside down and my whisper was that
other 'n' word ...as I watched HER child stand by HER side like an open
wound while she hung real low, I mean slow low dipping to a slow
motioned song in her head...the walking dead...
but never falling indicating she had more drop to go, slipped long ago
from her golden throne but her princess with a single snotty tear line stain
guarded her side waiting for a dime from a kind stranger walking by...me.

But while exaMINING the broken gems felled from the crown peeks, I
recognized them family jewels...I took one step, dropped a 50 in the vein
splintered hand and walked slowly, tearfully gasping the princess's hand in
mine, heading home..to my home, on the block...a single whisper in a stare
between us...princess to auntie.
I got you now...hold on. And as she was the daughter of Lot anyway...and
before backward glances turned them all to stone and crumbled to dust in
lives passed away... she did turn back to look
but only once before forgetting she was reborn like a Phoenix from this
nightmare…
just a kid from the block....
a piece of coal in the ashes out ruins of the blocks lost souls.

My sister's child

Ameerah Shabazz-Bilal

I am afraid

I am afraid! I am afraid of success. I am afraid of responsibility. I am afraid of the expectations that have been placed on me. I am afraid of judgement and what "they" will think, afraid, fear hinders my gift of playing with words, paper, ink. I am afraid of being misunderstood. I am afraid of rejection, afraid of both professional and personal connections. I am afraid I won't be liked; I am afraid of being seen, I am afraid of what my fears block and what they will reveal, that I am a perfectly flawed and severely broken human being. I am afraid of being alone, I'm afraid of the unknown, I am afraid that if I open my mouth my inabilities will be highlighted and range of weakness shown. I am riddled with fear, it scares even me, yet, I am angry and annoyed I have allowed fear to get the best of me. I have wrestled, I am uneasy, I am restless, I am queasy. I have named and have listed my vulnerabilities hoping to relinquish it's gripping hold and it's power over me. But, with all that I have listed still omitting a few, my greatest fear is not doing what I was meant to do! Yes, I have written them down, my attempt at release, working daily as my courage increase. I will tackle each one, and by God's grace overcome. I am choosing to believe by speaking my truth, I have already won.

Larissa Rhone

A Corny Poem

(For my Sister-Friend-n -Cousin and Homies)

That Sister-friend-n -cousin and homey that knows all the mess you been in. Have all the stories that could bring you to an end. That sister-friend-n-cousin and homey you can call at 3 or 4am. That sister-friend-n-cousin and homey who light that fire in your dreams within. That sister-friend-n-cousin and homey that you speak to every now and then, and pick up with you again and again like time ain't a thang in any dimension. That sister-friend-n-cousin and homey friend who been there since the beginnin…

It's a given they'll be in a selfie pictures with you gray-haired, snag tooth n grinning   to the end.

Nzima Hutching

Yellow Flowers (for Nzima)

You are my muse
A mystical universe
Speaking to me in constellations
No relation
Yet a sister
Though introduction
Was a blister
My war wound
Is now a trophy
Cementing our destiny
Outlining our trajectory
Embedded on cheek
I was meek
And you were wild
And in love
While I was infatuated
Lives separated
Yet still connected
And written word ws our quest
Admiration from a distance
Joy at your persistence
And in an instance
I returned
Both our hearts burned by loss
A seat at the table
Led to conversation
And elated over written words
And access and artistic distress
And in a beam
You shared a dream
And vision was birthed
You be match
And I bastions of ethanol
Above a sea of obsidian stones
When left alone
We birth nations

Set souls ablaze
Make stagnant change phase
We are chocolate brown
Melanated royalty
We are gentle angel
And sword yielding hellion
Straight laced rebellion
Gray haired locs
And vocabulary glocks
Yellow Reeboks
And mismatched socks
Balanced scales
Or tipped and raising hell
We are daughters of the revolution
Cooking up solutions
Verbally seducing
Strategically attacking
Celebrating all that is black
High yellow to blue black
Hella bougie or slinging crack
From a welcoming smile
To a long teeth smack
Prim and proper to twerking goddess
Loose and free to extremely modest
Every kind of everything
And all that my people bring
I feel in your presence
The essence of the Motherland
In Queen momma's hand
Healing touch of embrace
Encasing your love

Always hold yourself in high regard
You are of the gods
Cloaked in galaxies
Crowned with the minds of the ancients
Cheeks swollen with joy
Coy, yet courageous

Humble but that hood root is advantageous
A sunflower
Tal and brown
My sister
Always down
My friend
Always around
My muse
Future bound

T'challa Williams

Withholding Owning

truths are subjective   I'm writing out   my version
my   perspective   my arty mind   the understandings on my   timeline

See my   crusted ova scars   beauty marks   needs
mysteries   desires n   crossfires
are all working   my written legacies   probably   until my demise
I might even   crash   procession lines

thinkin   to trash   the dash
and   throw up   scannable barcodes   on everythang sold
including my tombstone

Lawd have mercy on me   I pray that don't be   my   only upload

I stand here dancing alone   bathrobed   to Nina Simone Black Gold
she's questioning   where do time go

tryna wait   to get old to unload   the classic stories told   to grandkids
just another soul   to stop   writing my guilt
in poetic   crypted codes   not ready for the expose

stealing second chance   gotta withhold   the ownin   live the circumstance
I start   where I gotta begin   make it so   I win   to grin n live again

not afraid if   my story includes   or confuse
him   or her or   displeases   so n so
see it was no   **we**   or   they
only me   that came out   my mother's pussy   on my birthday

I own my original sins   the burdens   I asked for forgiveness
to dismiss   my sketchy   business   to save the leftovers within

I pray my distance   so not to get bitten again   and again
I am human   made with a mix of morals, flesh and skin

Nzima Hutchings

Back-Boning (For T'challa)

we need the lady wearing
red black n green
back-boning things
killing mediocrities
in melanated soulful dreams
looming her hat out of necessity
shaking up feminine fragility

screamin I came for the bacon
ya ain't hearing me
firing smoke halos
and revolutionary signals
from her soul n lips
sassy hands on hips
shocking S painted chest

Negress n Negroes   says
"she did it all without recess
with her six bambinos"
their brows n postures
ask   but how though?

she'll say *"I got to"*
It's not magic or theatrics
perhaps metaphysical
I don't know
it's never always easy
yet   it pleases me

I cry   in the dark
I know a thing or two
about a heavy heart

She's nobody's victim
her 3rd eye rolls
n sees who's true
and do what a
lady gotta do

T'challa my
Sistah Libra-en
I got you...
and all the T'challas

the ladies wearing
red black n green
back-boning things
in melanated souls
and dreams

Nzima Hutchings

A Love Poem Never Written

our   essence

never inscribed

on refined wood

or cotton twines

I never could

catch up to

outline or define

our run on lines

our living proses

note our   love notes

our free verses

haikus & rhymes

our remixes & grinds

lyrical truths

abstract harmony

or metaphorical theories

endless stanzas

hyperboles   line breaks

and midnight onomatopoeias

or publish our poetic pauses

the lips to forehead kiss

the 8,760 days

since the fall of 96

Nzima Hutchings

I'm Free

Darkness falls

Thunder strikes

Cloudy skies

Darkest nights

Rain falls

washing debris

Yes Lord

yes, I'm

finally, free

Shakira D. Greene

Moth to Butterfly

The chrysalis fully opened
only after a life she birthed butterflied

mothering a few from her womb
taught her to nurture all
but the whole of her

she mothed about
unknowing her name
or span of her wings
tiptoed on life's edges
flown   a little clipped
but without regrets

though occasionally she wept
and rested on sunflowers
ruminating over un-flown flights

After a life she birthed butterflied
she gained this anew
bittersweet strength
shucked off
old wrappings n wings
ushered out a new purpose

some say a metamorphose

an unimagined recourse

something a mother

should never have to do

to carry on the flight

of her baby butterfly

that butterflied away

she vowed too flutter

in the throws

of this role

until she too

butterfly away

Nzima Hutchings

269 Lyme St. (For Nana)

we be sharing Hershey Kisses
tossing out almonds
sharing smiles n   milestones
sitting on old fashioned painted radiators
practicing multiplication facts

at 5 O'clock in the morn   you'd be reminded
That Nana came from a different kinda stock
Sunday morning you'd be smellin and awaken to
bacon and eggs n home fries   collard greens
macaroni and cheese   all at the same time
New Jennies on the block don't know nothing about that
it wasn't a mystery why alarm clocks were unnecessary

in the middle of the day at any given time
Nana would be watching The Jefferson's
drinking ginger ale or country time.

She loved scary movies too
but at times   she'd fall asleep
and we Grands and Greats
be wanting to hang and brave
so we start the tapping saga   and inquiry calls
"Nana Nana"   "Nana Nana "
Are you sleepin?   then there's the parting of
the top and bottom eyelashes and lids
and the dazed stare   and in a savior like breathy low tone
Nana would say "I'm not sleep   I'm resting my eyes.

Nana knew   and loved her children and grands
She'd let us stretch out   twirl and flex
not too much   but enough to grow
and learn
she gave wings to her children to sturdy us   as she studied them.
We acted out our fresh and brand-new innocence
as kids do   and she   let us be   just that   a kid   and protected that.

Her warm momma bear make it all betta hugs
and words   wisdom filled   along with grace

accompanied with fierce black lady magic like powers
made a generation or two   believe
she really had eyes on the back of her head
she seems to know everything   caught everything

Nana had given   and   popping hands.
See she kept an abundance of temptations
in her bedroom
peppermints butterscotch   all sorts of candies
the traditional gramma got candy thang   was ah thang
she wasn't havin greediness though
if you tried to steal it   she'd bite you   trust me I know

Nana loved her family hard
She'd press her lips tight   and be ready to fight if you messed with any of
hers.
She handled going up to the schools and taking care of business.

Education was important to her   she would gleam when one of hers made
the Dean's list.
Time grew on her   but her energy remained the same
for her grands and great-grands too.
She'd flex her life carrier of teaching and knowing the
system
correcting mistakes and schooled teachers.

At 269 Lyme in and outside, Nana showed us a buffet of love
The kinda love that if you thought you ran out of it   she'd give you more
There was tough love   unconditional love   family love   and sistah love
Mothering love   loyalty in the name of love in honor of Big Daddy
our Granddaddy   that ill nurse you   better kinda love
the stay with ya old fashion love   real love
love for community   spiritual love   self-love   and going to BINGO
love

Nana opened her doors too many   never minding dynamics
to whom ever needed it   she held herself and   her house rules to a
standard
if ya didn't obey you probably couldn't stay.

Nana real keepings   were un-bought and unedited

yet diplomatic and unapologetic   but unsullied by ego
what you see is what you get... She owned herself.
Traveling, teaching, bowling, being a member of clubs and churches
ordering Mr. pizza or gettin Giant Grinders, and going to bingo
was one thing...
but her mothering, praying and intimate conversations or watching her
watch Kings of Kings, truly celebrate life
or watching her sit in deep thought   was something else... ethereal like.

Nana was a living legend.
Games were made in her name.
Bootchie   Ms. Campbell   Nana Mommy   Mary
as kids we knew not to call her out of her name.
We even had a   " I dare you call her Bootchie game".

Nana, aunty, and mommy remember when stories were heavy already,
Now even more since February 2nd

We loved our Nana deeply...
But never did we love how hot   she kept her
room

or how loud she played The Sound of Music over the last few decades...
But I dear to say
I wouldn't mind feeling that heat
or hearing the sound of music song, once again with
her
Doe a deer...a female deer.... Ray   a drop of Golden sun...
Me   a name   I call myself

Nana was indeed a ray of light.

Nzima Hutchings

Call

I've been yearning to hear your voice

Just, hearing you say anything would be nice

Longing for your words of wisdom

The ones that keep me up thinking all night

I tried to pick up the phone & dial, but tears started rushing before I could dial the area code

Now I'm back in the corner sobbing again, back to this depressing mode

Just call me.

Tell me you're okay.

Tell me God is with you, and you watch over us every day.

Let me know you still remember us; you love us the same.

Just call me one more time mommy

I just need to hear your giggle, to feel your smile.

I know it doesn't make sense, but since I lost yours, mines been gone awhile.

Shakeela Dawn

I Cooked Breakfast Today

I cooked breakfast today,

Simple enough to do you say

Naw   not for me,

mind body and soul just won't let me,

Pain so unreal

So dark and deep

A love shared so passionately,

let's me know, okay I will be

I cooked breakfast today

Shakira D. Greene

When She Sees Me

As my mother's smile blossoms across her face
She turns toward the sun warming the glass of her window

She turns slowly
As her curving lips lift her cheeks, she blushes with rays of affection

Her eyes crinkle in the corners where happy crows landed years ago
To draw the smiles and laugh lines of her life

A satisfied, contented smile
Wide, closed mouth
Fed by sweet memories that light her eyes and radiate her entire face and body

She sits tall
Chin raised, neck stretched, looking up
As if reading clouds   Aaah, so grateful

I am her child and find myself
Thinking of countless times with her
Girl to woman times,
Daughter to mommy times,
Sharing our days as lovers, divorcee, widows
Hetero, lesbian, bisexed, black, proud
Christian, Buddhist, doubting and believing

Always belonging to her and she to me
Aaah...So many reasons to smile

Regina S. Dyton

Reciprocal fills

Filling up my empty and open spaces
with organic and positive energy
from outside into the inner and outer edges
of myself in my open spaces
and
filling in and out empty spaces
with my organic and positive energy
from the inner and outer edges of myself
into open spaces...outside.

Nzima Hutchings

Who?

Whose hair are you
 pullin?
Whose pussy are you
licken
body flipin?
whose back are you
arching
thighs n legs
are you   quivering
sqeezin ?
Who are you
pleasing
readin?
Who's getting
Part of It all
making the fall
of my tears
seem law
my nerve endings
crawl?
Tell me
whose gettin'
my call?

Nzima Hutchings

Words Will Never Hurt You

Sticks and stones
May break my bones
But words will never hurt me

At least that's what I was told
Before I grew old
Enough to know better
Before a boy had the audacity
To tear up my love letter
Back when I swung from trees
And could honestly blame the gravel
For the blood dripping
From my skinned knees

Those were simpler times
Times of nursery school rhymes
Sang at recess
Still stuck in the recesses
Of my aging mind
I remember when
I used to sing all the time

And skip, skip, skip to my loo
And you'd call your mama
To ask if you could come too
Back then the words didn't divide
We lived with arms open wide
Singing a shared anthem of childhood
All throughout the neighborhood

We played kickball in the court
And every other kind of sport
Boys and girls
Black, brown, and white
Played until the streetlights
Came on at night

At home in my bed
I'd recall that they've said

That I should:

Row, row, row my boat
Gently down the stream

But so rapidly
The water got so rocky
That my boat sprung a leak
And even the knees of superheroes
Went weak
When the mean girls
Would open their mouths to speak

Merrily, merrily, merrily, merrily
Life is but a dream

Only the words
Spoke the language of nightmares
No more skipping through life
Without a care
Not with them taunting me
About my clothes, my skin, my hair
So many places I yearned to go
But my boat couldn't take me there

Sinking, I was sinking
Right around the time the kids
Started drinking
And smoking weed
And keeping track of who had
And who hadn't done the deed
But I wasn't really up to speed
I had already seen too much
My body cringed at every touch

But they said:
Sticks and stones may break my bones
But words will never hurt me

Hey, Afro

Didn't you know
You look like Michael Jackson
Are you a boy or a girl?
Don't look so mad
I'm just askin'
Hey what are you anyway
Was that your white mom
And Black dad who picked you up today?

Say
You're tall
You must play basketball
You're quite a know-it-all
What do you call yourself?
You don't fit on any shelf
You move with stealth
Defying definition
And every premonition
Of who we thought you'd be

Twinkle, twinkle little star
How I wonder what you are
Up above the world so high

Your light scattered
Like diamonds in the sky
As you wondered why
You ever let words hurt you
The one thing you were told
That they never could do

Paige Vaccaro

~Tanka Poem~

Nina Simone Spinning Me

Dancing alone   all

grown   to Nina Simone   lit

feeling like I need

a little sugar in my

bowl   Black Gold   all in my soul

Nzima Hutchings

Make Love

I can't make love
Conform to my desires
She has a mind of her own
She's anything but submissive
Even when I get aggressive
She is dismissive
She leaves me wearing the collar
Idly whipping myself
Reminding me that no one will
If I can't love myself

I can't make love
With materials raw
Gleaned from all the pain
That continues to gnaw
Away at my hands
That grab and clutch
Fighting to hold onto
What hurts so much

I can't make love
Without the recipe
Even if all the ingredients
Lie waiting deep inside me
An array of useless things
Dance when pulled
By the connected strings
But that's not love
Just because my body sings

I can't make love
Where I want it to exist
No matter how hard I persist
I know it doesn't look like this
Or move like that
Love doesn't have to tell me
I already know the facts
Love is not a matter of opinion
She alone holds
The reigns of dominion
My heart lives and dies
Her minion

Paige Vaccaro

Broken and Replanted

broken branches

broken limbs

burnt red

blood-stained hair

dried leaves

of   late fall

the white beast

came cold

stole

tried to kill all

tortured

beat

shot

raped

but did not kill them all

the broken

the blacks n browns

the unbroken

the brave

the rocks n seeds

rerouted n replanted

bloomed

fought

tried

transitioned

lit skies

became the red

the moon

a guide

survived

Nzima Hutchings

Seconds Clean

They be clapping

Sayin and celebrating your
Years clean...yay

You did it!!

I sit silent with applause inside my eyes

Clap
clap
clap

Each clap like thunder
Rippling with my heartbeat

Here's to you
You with your underlying abuse

 freedom

Here's to me...

Cause I'm still walking around with this monkey on MY back
Yet YOU be free

I'm Still caught in chains
Of burnt-out pain

Mom, I haven't been freed

I'm still tied to leaning poles
Holding the geometry of life by the angled side

90 degrees of childhood lost
Non tilted straight up rays of Madness!

I hold on to the angles of spent realities

Reality

To keep THEM from falling
And catching my tears as they slide
Down poles, dipping but not hitting earth...ever

But I'm strong

I have the strength
Of a child's essence
Of burnt in fortitude
Of being silenced
Of tears ..that run inside
Of fear
Of no way of showing love...Without showing hate
Of self
Of fear
Of you returning

To HER

The monster
Of my youth
She still hides under beds
In closets
In the threads of my worn out knees

I suck in snot wells
Through black holes that should be eyes with souls
Dripping leaving paths
Paths uncovering coal shavings
Which cover my heart

When I'm allowed to breathe
I choke
I choke up you

I Fear seeing leaning poles
Cause they remind me each and everyone of them of you

Endless corners with cans, EBT cards, newspapers, kids clothes... mine
Selling them for crack, not food...

Mom, I'm zero minutes
Zero days
Zero Months
Zero years

free

No, no one freed me

I sit in silence
While you are praised

Weak ass'd excuses
For my hell

I stood silent thru it all
Where's my applause...

My award of a super f'd up life
That taught me 2 things

How to not to die
And how to fight ...

For life

When hands lift
And before they meet again
Vibrating sounds which creep into my coal mine of a heart

You glance at my silence

It holds secrets
Its clap like thunder
With the strength to
Crack and break through silence
So I see how you might be scared

Scared for me to speak

We are grateful we made it

Made it past late evenings
Of street walks
2 am freedom calls
Missed class trips
Deep nods thru parent meetings
Yours...

Those gold stockings with holes
You wore to pick me up from school...well at least you came

And that Afro matted wig you wore
To my graduation
Smelling like a spilled drink
Drinks of salvation

The fights I'd get into
After kid snickers about you

The hunger
For food and a life
The pain
Of being a child from the temporary motherless clan

Your skeleton frame
Your toothless grin

My never new clothes
My unkept 6 yr old self

Your screams thru playground
Fences at my lunchtime recess
Me pretending not to know you

My missed school days
My smells, yours too

My reflection in mirrors
Hoping not to become you

My screams the day they took
Me from school in that black car
From you..
black clouds of thunder scared,

left lonely last night and the other night and the other
when you didn't come home for me

8 years of foster care
12 years of blank black stares
20 years clean
20 nights of tears and heart screams

My 20 years of living me

Without you

I hear the claps and congrats
And I smother the rage within
Warming the coal deep within begging to take place to form MY diamond

It's like the irony of saying happy birthday to the child when the mom
bore the pain

Except mine is in reverse

They be clapping

I be sitting silent

Waiting...for the encore

Waiting for my applause

Princess Peaces
Ameerah Shabazz-Bilal

Yellow Dress for Her

Before I stood there in my yellow butterfly like, kaftan dress for her.
I gave it all that I had.   Bowed and agreed to the whole get up and go thing;
live on thing,   pretend she is there thing.   Considered taking a leap by
walking in her shoes…her silver metallic two or three-inch-high heel
prom shoes. The ones she wore once. But remembered n deemed her being
more graceful,   physically balanced,   fancier and braver than I.   Besides
she wore a size nine.   Think her spirit gave me a side-eye,
then laughed with me and at me.   I felt it.   As usual, somehow it all turned
into a cry.   Salty tears crowded my eyes, soaked up my cheeks and
collarbone. Sounds of howls took up residence in all my empty spaces.

My-my inner negotiator worked desperately to hold and save me...
The soliloquys and replays; and *okay-okay!!…okay? Okayeees… and
some other onomatopoeias* gave way. Time silenced and rounded the
clock. It was time to do the live thing. My-my toes stretched open,
my foot   slipped in and   settled into my gray flip flops.
My hands joined in…started wrappin my locs   favorably and delicately
in shiny satin. Then I stepped out… accepted my reward
tasted a moment   assembled grace.
Organically smiled and cried inside too.   Onlookers never knew   they
never do.   I make it picturesque.   Took the picture.
Stood there arms wide open, in my yellow butterfly like, kaftan dress
for her.

Nzima Hutchings
In loving memory of my daughter Knia K. Hutchings

My Message to Men

Men the silence that you give your woman when she asks you a question while you stare into your mobile device is, you're failing as a partner. The lack of eye contact when she is talking to you, trying to converse in an intellectual conversation in hopes to get your feedback, or opinion bestows a disconnection of her heart.

You can't hear past the distraction in your mind if your life is so focused on the illusions of the world. You cannot see the realism of the woman that has been placed in your life, if you are focused on the illusions of the women that are flashing past your news feed without stretchmarks, cellulite, small sculptured waist, big bottoms, perfect hair, flawless skin, long extended lashes, full lips, eyes that capture your soul by that stare looking back at you.

But you have the mother of your child, bearing the marks on her stomach, and thighs, the flap of extra skin from being stretched out carrying your son or daughter for 9 months. You have the hair that maybe has not been washed today, because she had no time, or was too tired after feeding the baby, getting the kids ready for school, cleaning, cooking, laundry, homework, practices, games, picking up after you, being your mother at times, because you fail to take initiative and step in when she is overworked, even possibly after working her 40-hour week on top of all of that. Is she not the Woman that should be looked at as your "Super Women". Hypnotized by the possibilities that arise in your mind created a disconnection with the only ability to see who is in front of you. Keep her on your side "Fellas" she will slip through your fingers like time, the time that you wasted not loving her and you have lost her to a GOD that she will fall so in love with you will no longer matter. GOD'S loyalty, his guidance, his presence in her life, the way he will cater to her every need, answer every prayer, and fulfill her every desire. The sweet nothings that GOD will whisper in her ear when she is discouraged, in despair, in need of a loving touch. When you woke up this morning and reached over and grabbed your mobile device and said Good morning to everyone whose picture you just double tapped making them aware that "You see them". When you should of reached over grabbed your woman by the waist and rolled her next to you, greeted her with a forehead kiss, and a good morning with that sweet aroma of morning breathe, but just know that "GOD" wakes her up with a sweet 'Good morning my precious Queen" I have given you another day to be great. No need to worry about the catering of MAN, GOD GOT YOU.

It is time Men begin to realize that when a Women falls in love with Jesus, he has lost her forever, but he has also blessed her Life, because his in actions guided her back to him who so loved her more than MAN can ever love her.

Miosotys Santiago

Truth Be Told

If you take a machete and
slash your momma door
that should have been a sign...

When your mama lives in a
house not a housing project
and she said her husband
promised her more that should be a sign.

Traveling down a road twice a week
to fenced in place of humiliation
and it's not your crime
when you should be college-bound
committed to a getting a PhD degree
that should be a sign

When your teenager and your child's
father left you at three months pregnant
and your daddy brings you your craving
that should be a sign.

Struggles get real when your
child is called to glory
and your God chosen one to
nurture her children and
suitcases are packed in the
closet for the escape
that should be the sign.

Can you tell me why I revisited
pain thinking that you would
help me nurture something you
knew nothing about
your pain was

deeply rooted in abuse... you didn't
get the lesson of a man uplifting
his daughter
that should have been the sign.

My daddy told me they aren't
worthy of my daughter
his wisdom should have been the sign
This is my truth!

Rosalyn Williams-Bey

A SMALL PIECE OF ME

Are those the keys I hear in the door at 3 a.m.? Here we go again, what's going to happen now, will I be able to sleep peacefully or will I have to hear that familiar name being spoken over and over again, (BITCH, BITCH, BITCH, BITCH, BITCH, BITCH, BITCH, BITCH, BITCH, BITCH, BITCH, BITCH, BITCH, BITCH) ...

I really began to question at times (was this really my name)?   I do not remember ever being called this as a child growing up or by anyone else in my life...But for some reason, this was the name he had chosen for me. I wonder why, I worked full-time, took care of our children, kept the house cleaned, clothes cleaned, meals cooked, hell I even kept myself nice, clean, hair did...but for whatever reason this was just not enough, what the hell did he want from me?

Well, it appeared to be quiet so far, did that mean you wanted to go straight to sleep or have sex with me and I hoped it would not be forcefully. As I waited and listened praying to God silently, I would not once again have to go through bullshit
and figure out how to protect my kids from hearing any of this...

All I wanted was to be able to go to work in a few hours, rested and not feeling anxious, tired, or upset due to "what happened to me" whatever that was. I was tired of having to call out of work because I was so emotionally drained and couldn't bear to perform my job which I loved... no one to talk to I thought would understand me and not judge me or make me believe there was something wrong with me like you tried to do. There was so much deceit and mistrust, from some family & friends, those supposedly close to me were right there co-signing your bullshit, feeding your ego, hanging out with you and
entertaining your female friends... but then smiling in my face like everything was good even though
they knew me, but would still easily smile in my damn face and say sis what's good, in my face really?

Cost me a really good friendship because "she" thought I knew what was going on in her relationship, but I didn't.
People wonder why I stayed away a lot, let me tell you it was because I refused to be one person sometimes, then another person at other times, being honest and true to myself always

suited me better. As I think back over my life some things, I had little control over changing, but staying with you WAY TOO LONG, I should have left that toxic demeaning relationship so long ago. What did I allow my children to experience, when walking away could have saved them any hurtful memories.

I hate myself for not being strong enough to walk away. We were way too young to try this thing called life
together, we had a child, got married, were responsible for raising another child. I had a miscarriage, then had another child, all the while trying to juggle being a wife, mother, cousin
daughter, sister and friend to others. The parts of myself I kept hidden, in order to move one foot in front of the other each day.

Did I ever wish I could not be here and ask God repeatedly why am I going through this? The answers are YES & YES,
but my babies were more important to me than allowing YOU to steal my joy, peace and happiness. You are one of two regrets I have in my life, but you are also a part of the best things in my life which are my children. I also regret not listening to. My Mother the many times she told me "something is not right with that boy" But as a young girl You think with your heart and body until you are mature enough to think with your mind and listen to your gut. Oh, life does have a way of teaching us. I know I am not the only woman in the world who has had negative experiences and heartbreak, but this is my story and I get to tell it on my terms with no apologies, this is my healing, this is for me. When you wonder what is behind these eyes of mine you will be able to see. Even though I love hard, I have been hurt deeply repeatedly and God has opened my heart so now I write to tell you why I am a special kinda lady named Kim.

Kimberly Johnson

UNMAKING

You were conceived in mud

and leaves and slug covered

pavement.

with slapped cheeks stinging and

eyes closing from a stranger's punch

and leftover redness from a knife pressed

into a young neck.

The smell of his dirty body and the

heavy pressure of youthful

legs being ripped apart and the

searing pulsation of your

unwelcomed life being

thrust into me.

And when it was over, it began

I lay moaning in dirt,

vision blocked by a ripped shirt

Jacked over a sweaty head and yet you still had the

audacity to travel onward.

Why didn't the bloody darkness scare you?

When I finally could stand

millions of your companions

released themselves and slid down my bruised legs.

Why didn't you?

And when your stranger-father

said-

> If you tell-I'll kill you,
>
> Why didn't you know you weren't wanted and slide
>
> out as a puddle of gross
>
> white ooze?

And when I found one someone

to tell and no one believed,

you did not stop

> your pursuit of my womb.

So I played mute

> and hoped you'd go away.

I told no one else and

spent my days in listless stupor.

While replays of your foul

> conception taunted my memory.

Weeks began to pass and

with them the steady

> Boom/boom/boom/boom iambic

beat of your ill-gotten heart

grew stronger.

> And I began to
>
> Imagine I smelled you

damp and lingering like

the after taste of garlic.

Except it never wore off the

vampire-

      who moved in me like a squatter and left his trash behind.

So, I went thru the days

feeling the end of my

youth expanding in front

of me

-wishing for a way to save my life.

I could hold it in no more

      -so I shattered my silence

      and let my raped anguish out.

Take this vile monster from I cried

-the world was silent and still I screamed as

I imagined this thing growing

spindly hairs and fangs

which it could use to pierce my heart.

I screamed and finally

the angels of mercy,

In their long white coats

and white white walls

layed me down on the

cold white tomb with wheels.

I wanted out like Lady Macbeth- her damned spot.

Once again your entrance

to life was ripped

open but now I yielded,

and the angels told me

to count backwards from a hundred.

And I was dead.

And the exit you would not make

on your own

was made for you.

  You clung to life I was told

  but the angles were stronger.

It was a bloody bloody feud

fought with high speed full vacuum armor.

And when an angel touched

  my sweaty brow,

wet with labor's glow

I rose from the dead

and looked to the floor.

And there you were

  -a bloody mass entombed in a glass jar.

And I laughed to be free of you.

Leslie Bivans

Every Kinda Lady II

I am one lady, yet every kinda lady. I am that lady on the carpet praying on her knees. The same lady that'll come packing if you mess with her babies. I am the lady they call to make the macaroni n cheese and collard greens that need no hot sauce   who tries to feed all. I am that same lady unashamed to go commando while wearing kaftan gowns, mom jeans n Afrocentric wraps…run outdoors with socks   mismatched.

I am one lady, yet every kinda lady, an "I'll be just fine kinda lady," with full-grown lady test   doing her best.

Ah let a *motha fkr* know kinda lady   when I'm on my give no f---kness… holding my hands over my heart   warning   don't mess with this.

I am one lady, yet every kinda lady. The one for a minute who played the fool, gave of herself   way to soon   been renamed   baby momma. The same lady who say   "I's be married now"   like foreva eva   eva eva.

I am one lady, yet every kinda lady that make the other ladies comfortable. The lady they call to relay their right n wrongs.

Like "*I did what a sistah had to do to keep my lights on*"

The "I tried it only once"   same ole song
flipped food stamps and snap cards stories

the "I'm winning at   life's mysteries

the escape plan from a man story

the Ossie Davis   n   Ruby Dee   love supreme
and doing it all while I can testimonies

I am only one lady, yet every kinda lady. Walking unedited is my testimony. I am that kinda lady that dance alone in the kitchen to Nina Simone, singing I want a little sugar in my bowl   burn sage, drive down highways screaming and daydreaming   connecting soul 2 soul

to get "*back to life   back to reality" to* be well in my own Black fragility.

Not a mad hatter   but just one lady   with a sundry   of hats…

Yet, I do solo tea parties at high noon and share poetic justice on open mics. Talks in circles and slide down deep rabbit holes.

Imagining cafes and rocking gardenias in my locs like, Billie Holiday *singing "Ain't Nobody Business if I Do"* and sharing conversations with Tupac about our dear momma   and chopping it up wit   Zora n Du buios on this twoness   and maintaining all this   lady-ness   with three Black sons.

I am one lady, yet every kinda lady creating her own retreats n cheat sheets...polishes her toes only in the summer   but keeping-em soft n smooth daily. Eat crunchy peanut butter straight from jars with her finger, showers at 3 in the morn to rid emotional thorns... the kinda lady that throws her grands on her hips and sings lullabies and   don't you dears with gummy bears in hand   rollin both prayers and curses from her lips

I am one lady, yet every kinda lady that wears her melanin deep, loves the skin she's in...but the same lady that wishes her butt just didn't look like Karen's...The same lady who disclaims being a feminist, yet claims being everything womanist, a free lady, an unapologetic owning   all of her-story's kinda lady...

The glowing lady, tainted lady, the lady in red kinda lady, stupid in love lady, modest lady, boss lady, welfare, stylish, misused, and abused lady. A soulful, beautiful, sensual, laid-back kinda lady

the red   black n green lady   hustling lady   pioneering lady and down for her Brothas that can't breathe kinda lady...

The nurturing, broken, prolific n eclectic kinda lady, the giving to much lady   grieving lady   defeated and bounced back up kinda lady, savage lady, the other women lady, the I ain't got time for that lady   refined lady

Queen momma fresh baked chocolate cookies kinda lady, football and dance mom lady, worn the hell out lady   the acquiescent lady, respected lady, delicate and resilient kinda lady.

The kinda lady that writes, life's snippets and chapters on blank spaces...from broken to straight lined paper   to pages.

The kinda lady that knows when to whip out   the kinda lady she needs. The lady that can't wait to greet every kinda lady she'll be... The kinda lady that just love being an authentic kinda lady.

Nzima Hutchings

13-And Today...Everything Changes!

In a sea of tears
Seeing and feeling
All the chipped away pieces of my heart
A heart so big
Loving
Nurturing
Full of compassion

How could you do this to me
Over and over again
And you never even apologized

YOU left me
feeling unworthy of love & affection
YOU left me
feeling like a failure as a woman wife & mother
YOU left me
feeling guilty for wanting support for me and my
Royalez YOU left me
feeling used for sex & my spirit
YOU left me
feeling disrespected & disregarded
And Then There's YOU
YOU that started all of this
Cuz YOU JUST LEFT
And kept leaving
over and over again
first a season
then a year
a lifetime
and then eternity
YOU left me
to be in this world without you
without them
without
love
support

protection
back up
YOU left me
feeling that I could trust
that you
and them
would always leave me

Until Today
because Spirit whispered to me
thru my tears
that it's time
time to nest
with love
with support
with protection
with backup
In preparation to FLYY!
Cuz YOU never apologized
THEY never apologized
BUT HE DID...
HE apologized for YOU & ALL the
rest HE affirmed that
MY VOICE Matters
MY GIFTS Matter
I Matter...

So...I AM
GATHERING
up all the chipped away pieces of my
heart MIXING
them with the light of Spirit
CREATING
a healing blend of freedom &
love POURING it into my heart
FILLING in all the places of leaving

And Now
From this day forward
With my

Healing
Loving
Nurturing
Compassionate Heart

I AM
taking responsibility for my part in
this forgiving myself
forgiving you and all of them
freeing me up
to love myself even more
And Today...Everything
Changes!

Anyangō Yaa Asantewaa

"Land of Milk and Honey" Sticky Honey

Legs spread like condiments,
he closed his eyes and slowly inhaled her sweetness.
Laying his head on her left pillowy thigh he got comfortable, his lips met
hers with soft grazing.
Tongue tipping, circling, licking, indulging her clit head.
Sticky honey oozed, it was candy for breakfast, she moaned.
Spreading her lips apart, tongue dove in for a delicious ride,
Grabbing his head and her legs wrapped into a pretzel, whispering "Go
deeper, I want to feel you on the inside".
As he obeyed her commands her body convulsed, legs closed in choking
his head but he didn't stop because he knew her sweet, milky, gushiness
was on its way.
He obliged...

Hillary Brown
~honeyB~

Ode to Private Party

Flying solo
On my dolo
Alone and full, you know?
Satisfied by my flaws
Accepting of physical inconsistencies
Hell, I'm a mystery
And being alone to solve me
Is epiphany

T'challa Williams

Linda J. Greene (Aunty-Mom)

Aunt Lin more than my kin, you were my auntie-mom
my friend to the end
You hated your middle name so I would pretend to feel the same
Josephine Josephina   all I could think of
is Ms. Baker and I love her
Thinking of you and our hair tales
you'd pull my hair gently singing
Choo choo go the trolley   Choo choo go the trolley
Neva will I forget us   and our, once upon a time favorite song
Aunt Lin I want a cornbraid going down the side
wait no how about a ponytail to the side
can I wear my hair out in the back for the first day of school?
A bang in the front too?
Thinking of you and the cigarette derail   you busted me and my crew
chew chew on the ciggy   chew chew on the ciggy we were threw
Never did I smoke a cigarette again
Thinking of you when I thought I wasn't a virgin   you and Auntie Dear
gathered around me like honey bees coming to love n sting me
just to fine I didn't understand nothing about doing the do
Thinking of you   when I ran from a fight
you gave me the ole shoo shoo   told me to never bolt from a fight
and better get it right   or you were gonna handle me   needlessly to say
I learned quickly   to set up and posture right
I thank you   life's punches came for me
met me throwin jabs I took my losses   I bobbed and weaved made wins
Thinking of you on the day my heart was broken
you came threw traveling miles to see me through   you were gansta
a hat I never seen you wear before   I swear you were the very first
Every Kinda Lady   my mind can report
Thinking of you being there   and there and there   and there and there...
even with me   to have my first born   my own little boo boo
you held my hand in the birthing room   I could never forget you
you had my back   always freely no matter who Godzilla   or my daddy
in all life's turns and travels while calling me Flora Bell
and literally riding rails   with me
choo choo go the trolley   choo choo go the trolley

Nzima Hutchings

Honey Loved

6-HONEY LOVED!

You Know How I Know I'm Honey Loved?
I Can Feel I'm In Your SoulBliss…
As You Sip & Savor Me…
With An Undying Thirst…
Only I Can Quench
Over & Over…And Over…

You Know How I Know I'm Honey Loved?
I Can Feel You FLYYING IN…
Joining In…
With The Wind Underneath My Expanding Wings… My
Desire…Becomes Your Desire…
To FLYY Higher…

You Know How I Know I'm Honey Loved?
Our Minds Meet…
In An Unspoken…Understanding…
Of the Purposeful Pain…
Thru My Seasons Of Privilege & Poverty…
You Look Into My Eyes…
The Windows To My Soul…
You See It All…
And You Hold Me…
At The Ground…
Knowing I Will Rise…

You Know How I Know I'm Honey Loved?
When I Move…You Move…Just Like That…
In Perfect Unison and Harmony…
Our Movement…Flawsome…
Our Missed Steps…Effortlessly…Blend Into Our Flow… And We
Simply Keep Moving…
Feeling Our Way…
From My Heart To Yours…
Returning In An Endless Circle…

And You Know What??!!

In My Season Of Prosperity…
On My Path Of Abundance & Growth…
I AM…
WORTHY & DESERVING…
Of..
Your HONEY LOVE…

Why??!!
Cuz I've Had Enough Motherfuckin' Vinegar…
To Last a Lifetime!!!
You Feel Me??!!

Anyangō Yaa Asantewaa

Brave Space

Broken like shattered glass from the mirror. Reflections of who I want to be.
Dreams delayed feeling like they are so far from my reach.
Broken is what life has been for me.
Comforting the little girl in me.
Looking for the Brave Space in me.
Walking toward my destiny.
Recognizing the uniqueness in me.
Learning to live my best life and becoming the Fabulous me.

Rosa M. Bailey

~ Motivation ~

Your Words

Your words are your power. They flow from your head,
through your heart, and your hands onto the page. You have control of
your universe, and your words not only matter, but give hope, courage,
and resolve to all who read them.

Marilynn S. Turner

Quotes & Writing Prompts

Wild fires have no form, just like emotions are without shape...

(Respond to this quote)

_____

_____

_____

_____

_____

_____

_____

_____

_____

_____

_____

_____

_____

_____

_____

_____

_____

_____

_____

_____

_____

_____

_____

Truths-holds no sympathy, acquaintances, hands, or lies...

(Respond to this quote)

_____

_____

_____

_____

_____

_____

_____

_____

_____

_____

_____

_____

_____

_____

_____

_____

_____

_____

_____

_____

_____

_____

_____

_____

_____

Daydreaming inwardly into your own heart will tell you how brilliant and how screwed up you are... (Respond to this quote).

_____

_____

_____

_____

_____

_____

_____

_____

_____

_____

_____

_____

_____

_____

_____

_____

_____

_____

_____

_____

_____

_____

_____

_____

_____

_____

_____

_____

Hard to believe those that bear untold stories or trauma don't have a witness. (Respond to this quote)

_____
_____
_____
_____
_____
_____
_____
_____
_____
_____
_____
_____
_____
_____
_____
_____
_____
_____
_____
_____
_____
_____
_____
_____
_____
_____

It is best to write the story before the storyline changes… What are you waiting for to tell your story? (Respond to this quote)

_____

_____

_____

_____

_____

_____

_____

_____

_____

_____

_____

_____

_____

_____

_____

_____

_____

_____

_____

_____

_____

_____

_____

_____

_____

_____

I leave post it notes on my bathroom mirror to remind myself never to compromise myself.

Write about a time that you felt that you compromised yourself...

_____

_____

_____

_____

_____

_____

_____

_____

_____

_____

_____

_____

_____

_____

_____

_____

_____

_____

_____

_____

_____

_____

_____

The wild naturally plant seeds and craft spontaneous garden.

Where would you like to be planted?

_____

_____

_____

_____

_____

_____

_____

_____

_____

_____

_____

_____

_____

_____

_____

_____

_____

_____

_____

_____

_____

_____

_____

Write your cocky honesty…

Write what you really just don't give a (*F*) about.

_____

_____

_____

_____

_____

_____

_____

_____

_____

_____

_____

_____

_____

_____

_____

_____

_____

_____

_____

_____

_____

_____

_____

_____

She wrote to the soul that was taken, given, needed and shelved...

(respond to this quote)

_____

_____

_____

_____

_____

_____

_____

_____

_____

_____

_____

_____

_____

_____

_____

_____

_____

_____

_____

_____

_____

_____

_____

_____

_____

_____

How you live in your open and closed spaces, comes back to you in your open and closed spaces. Can you relate?

_____

_____

_____

_____

_____

_____

_____

_____

_____

_____

_____

_____

_____

_____

_____

_____

_____

_____

_____

_____

_____

_____

_____

_____

_____

Hand me Down Roaches

(They say even when the world ends, roaches will still be here...)

Hand me down roaches are gross, ignorant, stereotypical, dysfunctional, and negative hard to kill beliefs... that are handed down from one generation to next. Often causing generational harm, adverse emotional trauma, insecurities and more.

Generate a list of your own.

If you heard, received or repeated any of these statements, you received a hand me down roach or handed one down to someone else.

Examples:

- ➢ Don't name your baby a black or ghetto sounding name.
- ➢ Pinch the baby nose to keep it from being flat or getting too big.
- ➢ Don't be out here showing your colors.
- ➢ You are brave for wearing your hair natural.
- ➢ Check the baby's ears, that'll let you know how dark the baby really gonna be.
- ➢ I think people who get life insurance on family are opportunist... they should be ashamed of themselves.
- ➢ She is cute to be dark.
- ➢ You betta go get yourself a real 9 to 5 job and forget about being an entrepreneur or self-made negro.
- ➢ Chile you need some sun and a sandwich

_____

_____

_____

_____

_____

_____

_____

_____

Mini Journal Space

How many ladies have you been in your life time???
Write out your puzzle pieces on the next 12 pages.

Loved Lady

Beautiful Lady

Prolific Lady

Pious Lady

Insecure Lady

Poetic Lady

Lady

Eclectic Lady

Savage Lady

Ego Trippen Lady

Hurt Lady

Risky Lady

Single Mom Lady

Dubious Lady

Free Lady

Boss Lady

EKL Co.

Surviving Lady

Lonely Lady

Angry Lady

Grieving Lady

Uninhibited Lady

Sick Lady

Peaceful Lady

Broken Lady

Queen Lady

Acquiescent Lady

Sad Lady

Super Woman Lady

Duplicitous Lady

Phoenix Lady

Bitchy Lady

Resilient Lady   Caretaker Lady

~ The Ladies of the Pages ~

~ *Lady Shakira* ~

Shakira D. Greene is a resident of Hartford, CT single mother of three. A graduate of Goodwin College. She works as a provider services analyst. In addition, Shakira is a member of toastmaster international, a volunteer for Hartford's L.I.T.; a literary organization. she enjoys reading and spending her spare time with her family.

~ *Lady Roni* ~

Roni D. Williams (now Roni D. Elamé), is and has always been a true RONaissance Woman. In her inspiring life journey, she has found success as an influential culture, fashion, entertainment, business, finance and lifestyle curator. Roni is a model, actress, corporate executive, author, and entrepreneur. She is the Founder and Principal of The Princess Trust, an elegant financial empowerment brand for women. Roni counts her role as a mother and a wife as her most important, and currently resides in Los Angeles, California, with her loving husband, son, and beloved furry babies.

~ Lady Ameerah ~

Ameerah Shabazz-Bilal is a visual artist from Newark, NJ with a unique talent of telling stories through poetry and Visual Arts. She is a Teacher, Writer/Author/Illustrator, Poet, and Photographer, founder/facilitator - "When Women Speak" and "When People Speak" - poetry platforms where creative voices are supported and empowered. Author of "Breathing Through Concrete".

Her mantra is: "Poetry isn't poetry unless it's Spoken...Word".

~ *Lady T'challa* ~

T'challa Williams: Executive Co-Founder, Spokeswoman, Chief Advisor, Project Manager of Hartford's L.I.T; CEO of Wright Ink Productions, Published Author, Actress, Poet; Community Activist, Chairperson of the School Governance Council for HPHS, Member of Greater Hartford Art Council; Board of Directors Artist and Advisory Committee

~ *Lady Lashawn* ~

Lashawn Henderson-Middleton: is a graduate of Andrew's University, Hartford's L.I.T. founding member and Commemorative Arts Award Official, Owner of Lashawn Bakes, Published Poetess, Diversity poet and social worker for The Village for Families and Children; Board Member of Journey Writer's Inc.

~ *Lady Narelle* ~

Narelle Thomas is a visual, performing and healing artist from Springfield, Massachusetts. She is also a published and self-published author and artist. Focusing on creating art and writing that has a voice of its own, working with her hands to make jewelry, plant based, herbal, and natural products, Narelle is never bored. Everything produced is seen as an opportunity to further create dialogue, aid healing, and insight transformation. www.Narelleakc.weebly.com

~ *Lady Lynette* ~

Lynette Johnson is a poet, a performing artist, a voice actor and an event host. She has published four collections of poetry and her most recent book was also a one-woman show; Supreme. Using poetry, Lynnette discusses relationships, injustice, God, love and unlove with a little humor and plenty of vulnerability. She looks forward to continuing to use her art to uplift and connect

~ Lady Tracy ~

If Sampson's strength was in his hair, Mind.Evolution.'s strength is in her voice! Since 2000, Tracy Caldwell has made a name for herself as Mind.Evolution. A lifelong resident of Hartford, CT; Tracy Caldwell is a powerful voice for women, the community and people of color. She represents the rose that grew from the concrete with her beautifully woven poems that display the resiliency, strength, and fortitude despite the challenges that are presented to deter her. Tracy's reflections on society and social justice are a call for attentiveness and action. Whether discussing body image, with her stage play The Thick Chronicles: A body Image Story, or the intersectionality of women's issues and people of color, in her books Bare Naked and Exposure, Tracy lays out the cost of these issues on us women and on society at large, inviting the audience to question assumptions and find ways to make a difference.

~ *Lady Hillary* ~

Hillary N. Brown aka "honeyB" is a wife, mother, student of life learning, works FT, 3x Entrepreneur, Meal Prep Chef, Wellness Empowerment Coach and last but not least an Erotica Poetess. Her nickname "honeyB." speaks to her sweet but busy nature to embrace whom she is in this lifetime, unapologetically comfortable, untamed and free to be. Hillary writes erotica to help others awaken and reconnect with their inner joy confidence, sexuality and sensuality. She is a firm believer in the power of human connection.

~ *Lady IfeMichelle* ~

IfeMichelle Gardin, is a Writer of fiction, prose and theater who has organized events and created events to showcase artists of the African Diaspora. She has worked as a Creative Writing instructor. Served as board member for several arts organizations, organized a great number of cultural events, including several Kwanzaa celebrations. Ife has worked in administration for several arts organizations in New Haven, CT and produced plays.

In addition, Ife worked with community based social service organizations in case management, as assistant director, coordinator and served as a board member. She is currently Founder of the Elm City LITFEST, a celebration of LITerary arts, LITerary Artists and LITerature of the African Diaspora

~ Lady Leslie ~

Leslie Bivans, MA, is a former law enforcement officer, turned writer, poet, actress and performance artist. She holds a Masters in English and Creative Writing and writes everything from Sci-fi erotica, poetry to children's stories. She can most often be found living life on the wild side where only people who still believe in unicorns live.

~ Lady Che 'La 'Mora ~

I Che' La'Mora Hardy is a creative artist, life coach, and author. I enjoy utilizing all of my talents to communicate with the world around me. I love painting, but I am more than a painter. I explore my talents through use of drawing, food, photography, poetry, music, dance, and writing. Art allows me to show who I really am with no restrictions. I can share my heart and soul with the world. I love expressing myself this way. One thing I love about art is that it touches you regardless of age, gender, language or culture.

~ Lady Na'Imah ~

Na'imah A. Muhammad,
Retired: Guidance Counselor, Master Hypnotist, and Doula
Presently working as a Personal Care Attendant for Interim Health Care
for homebound and disabled clients.
Finding and working on connecting the dots to historical migrations of
indigenous peoples and the erasing and removal of Tribal Nations lands
and culture.

~ *Lady Miosotys* ~

My name is Miosotys Santiago I am the founder of Exemplify to Edify, LLC a Women's Empowering Network. I am a Motivational Empowerment speaker not by any schooling, or Degree but solely by experience. I am a survivor of child molestation, teen rape, attempted teen suicide survivor, teen pregnancy, domestic violence, and a survivor of the 9/11/ attacks on September 11, 2001 having escaped Tower One.   I am humbled to have been graced the 2015 Essence Magazine Ageless Beauties article, a 100 Women of Color 2019 Honoree…

Published works: A Memoir titled God's Diamond, and Amazons Best-selling co-author in the, I AM MY STORY our Voices Anthology and Movement.

~ *Lady Larissa* ~

Larissa Rhone is the founder and CEO of Journey2Free and CEO/founder of L.H.R. Foundation. She is an advocate supporting victims of childhood sexual abuse and incest in the United States and Jamaica. She is a mom, writer and poet. She studied at Albertus Magnus College. She currently resides in the state of Connecticut, but is originally from Seaforth, Saint Thomas, Jamaica

~ Lady Kimberly ~

My name is Kimberly Johnson and I was born and raised in the North End of Hartford, CT. I am an Entrepreneur, a Licensed Professional Counselor focusing on mental health, addiction and trauma. I have always enjoyed reading and writing, also love spending time with my family and friends.

~ *Lady Paige* ~

Paige Vaccaro, from Long Island, New York, holds a B.A. in English from Rutgers University and a M.A. in Elementary Education from Johns Hopkins University. After 12 years of teaching in public schools in Baltimore, Brooklyn, Newark, and Ocean Township, NJ, Paige relocated to South Jersey. In 2016, Paige founded the nonprofit organization Communities Revolutionizing Open Public Spaces (C.R.O.P.S.), which hosts local farmers markets, community gardens, paid internships and educational programming and events. A born writer, Paige writes poetry, memoirs, short fiction, blogs, and co-hosts a virtual open mic called Black Poetry Matters.

Follow her on Facebook and Instagram @flybypoetry @plantaseed services @cropsnj

~ *Lady Jamilah* ~

Jamilah Rasheed owns three businesses; Shea by J, Amatullahs Books, Ventures Unlimited. Jamilah is also the author of the book "Jeddah Begins Every Day with Bismillah." She is also the director of a nonprofit, the New Haven Inner City Enrichment Center (NICE).

~ *Lady Maryam* ~

Author and Educator Umm Juwayriyah (Maryam A. Sullivan, M.A.) is a native of Springfield, Massachusetts. She is the pioneering author of Urban Muslim Fiction in 2006. Since then, Umm Juwayriyah has authored five fiction books for adults and children, edited three anthologies, and has staged two plays, one at Harvard and another at Yale University. Umm Juwayriyah is also a full-time teacher in Springfield, Massachusetts with a Master's degree with honors from Regis University.

~ *Lady Elizabeth* ~

Elizabeth Johnson is an up-and-coming Author, Experienced/Patient Care Coordinator and Certified Nursing Assistant. A New York City Native, graduate from Branford Hall Career Institute, Southington, CT. She obtained a certificate from Capitol Community College (Hartford, CT) as a Health Claims Specialist. Elizabeth is engaged in The Project Resiliency Movement as a Resiliency Bee. Elizabeth's motto "KEEP SHINING". She enjoys motivating others to SHINE like the diamonds they are, maintain a positive attitude while facing adversity, a show stopping model in the ground breaking plus size industry, and giving back in any way possible.

~ *Lady Regina* ~

My name is Regina Dyton, and I testify that Nina Simone and writing saved my life. It was my best option to self-harm, substance abuse or other treacherous response to trauma. It purges bad feelings and invokes meaning and joy. My public readings begin as a social justice advocacy tool. Helping people to feel someone else's experience fuels empathy that can motivate alliances for social action. In addition, I have written for and performed in plays on diverse platforms. Currently, I am a member of Journey Writer's, INC.

~ Lady Stephanie ~

Wife, Mother of III and Published Poetess Àsé

~ *Lady Rosa* ~

Rosa M. Bailey, aka CEO Boss Lady is a native of Hartford, CT. She currently resides in Bloomfield, CT. Her love of reading makes the library her favorite place to visit. She is a wife and the proud mother of three adult sons and four grandchildren. Ms. Bailey is the CEO of RMB Management Group, a full-service training and development center for aspiring entrepreneurs and leaders

~ Lady Shakeela ~

Shakeela Dawn is a poet, writer, and certified Doula.
Born and raised in Queens, New York, she is an advocate for women, and
supports Black Mental Health Awareness.

~ *Lady Marilynn* ~

Marilynn Turner is a Professor of English at Asnuntuck Community College in Enfield, CT where she teaches writing.
In addition to teaching at Asnuntuck, Turner has written for Connecticut Food and Farm Magazine, has read her original works at Confluencia, Naugatuck Valley Community College, and is currently editing a collection of essays for publication.

~ *Lady Desiree* ~

Desiree, also known as Doc Poetic Jewels, is an author and poet. She was awarded, Honoree of the 100 Women of Color in 2020.

~ *Lady Amalita* ~

Amalita van Buuren was the Former Program Coordinator for the Parent Leadership Academy. She studied Government and Economics at Smith College. She ran the Sunny Patch Garden for years in Enfield, CT . She currently lives in Arnhem, Netherlands and was originally from Eufaula, Alabama.

~ *Lady Rosalyn* ~

Rosalyn Williams-Bey hometown is Harford, CT. She is a Hartford Connecticut Transportation Counselor for, Capital Regional Education Council, and a member of Commission on Children. She is a lover of fashion, enjoys journaling and reading in her spare time.

~ *Lady Anyango* ~

Sistah Anyangō is the Founder and CEO of The FLYY Movement. She is a Dancer, Fitness Professional, Visiting Lecturer, Empowerment Freedom Coach, and Workshop Facilitator. Sistah Anyangō is an experienced instructor with over forty years in various dance mediums. Sistah Anyangō has also created events and programs in schools, community agencies, and institutions of higher learning. Recently she has implemented Workplace Wellness to help organizations create a Culture of Self-Care. Sistah Anyangō has been recognized and received an award by the following entities: Circle of Hands, Campaign for Peace, 100 Women of Color, You are Beautiful and When Destiny Meets Purpose

~ *Lady Asmaa* ~

Asmaa Kamara is a Muslim woman, mother, wife, educator, and poet. She enjoys inspiring people to be the best version of themselves and finding meaning in life; it is her true passion.

Our voices, our her-stories scribed into books are powerful... they are ours...our spirits, inner workings and imagination poured out onto paper...it belongs to us. Deeming it necessary to be told authentically by us...claimed, protected, and celebrated by us.

Submissions

Guidelines:

When submitting your piece(s) to **EKLanthology@gmail.com**, please ensure that the subject line reads: **Anthology submission and the year 20____.** Submitting outside of this email, may become lost or missed, and is not advised.

Submissions opens January 15th Annually Deadlines is March 15th

- Unpublished original piece(s)
- Standard 12pt. font, Times New Roman font, single space.
- Microsoft Word Doc. or goggle doc (no handwritten or typed)
- No PDF formats or photos will be accepted
- No simultaneous submissions
- No more than 3 submission
- Edited submissions only
- Please include a title for each submission

Please include your full name, preferred name for publication, a functional email address, any additional form of contact. Optional include a 3-to-5-line bio., a clear profile photo. Photos will be used for marketing and may be included in the anthology. If your piece is selected you will be notified. All submissions submitted in any given year may be considered for future publications.

Note: Submissions may appear on various, Every Kinda Lady dais...Such as, future anthologies, plays, podcast, social media lives, website, online blogs and more, crediting contributing author(s). No royalties agreed or negotiated.

Made in the USA
Coppell, TX
23 January 2021

48629366R00103